STRING
THEORY

POEMS BY
ROBERT C. COVEL

For Julia
I hope you enjoy my poems!
Dr. Bob
3 October 2012
"It All Connects!"

STRING
THEORY

POEMS BY
ROBERT C. COVEL

V

Vabella Publishing
P.O. Box 1052
Carrollton, Georgia 30112

Cover design by DianaBlack.com

Manufactured in the United States of America

13-digit ISBN 978-1-938230-11-0

Cataloging in Publication Data

Covel, Robert C., 1949-
  String theory / poems by Robert C. Covel.
    p. cm.
  ISBN 978-1-938230-11-0 (pbk.)
  I. Title.
  PS3603.L75S77 2012
  811'.6--dc23

                                              2012024780

10 9 8 7 6 5 4 3 2 1

Dedication

For my mother Ruth McClintock Covel,
who believed in me and made me who I am
and
my wife Deloris Covel
for her staunch support and constant love

Table of Contents

Love Knots

CONNECTIONS

String Theory

"The rose window of Chartre is in it
And Euclid's lines upon sand.
—James Dickey, "The String"

Cat's cradle, cup and saucer, made of string,
we weave the airy images of thread.
Our fingers pass the patterns back and forth,
entangled in the web our fingers weave.

Across the sky, the patterns of the stars,
like Indra's Net, the constellations whirl.
The cosmos cast upon a sea of black,
the slow and silent glide of galaxies,
as stars revolve in Fibonacci swirls.
From light years to millennia of light,
time warps and woofs the fabric of the stars.

The poets, saints, and scientists who search
for patterns in the network of the stars,
assign the numbers to connect the dots.
They hear the silent harmony of spheres,
describe the dance, the choreography
of light. The poet's rhythms intertwine
with scientific theories, heart and mind.

As Euclid's rule and compass measure space,
Pythagoras triangulates the stars,
creating geometric strings of thought.
Einstein and Newton's formulas compose,
in skeins of numbers, symphonies of thought.

From subatomic particles to space,

from tiny to immense, they interweave:
the luminescent threads of thought unite.
As particles in waves, the forces swirl,
creating patterns, on the cosmos cast.
Like fingers meditating, counting beads,
we seek illumination in the stars.

The string game plays itself with unseen hands.
As fractal patterns replicate themselves,
vibrations resonate across the strands.
A woven web, in wonder, intersects:
The universe is one—it all connects.

Stars

Gazing upward at the stars and moon,
I stand, gape mouthed, witnessing infinity.
The light from eons past pours down.
Light years beyond, I gaze into the past
at points of stars
and galaxies that whirl through
immensities of time.
The starlight penetrates my eyes;
I stand, not deaf, but dumb:
speechless, mute witness to the light.
Mouth open wide,
from Darl's dipper I swallow stars
and drink the Milky Way.

Seven Stars for Icarus
(For Christa McAuliffe)

I: Movement

More than Icarus, they dared the sun,
and not just the sun, but the stars.
They challenged Newton's laws,
dared to soar beyond human imagination,
beyond scientists' squared distances.
As they rose on a column of fire,
we shaded our eyes against the blaze.
We watched as they rose on wings
of fragile technology,
strained against the chains of gravity
and the past, looked upward and outward
to freedom and the future.
But our blaze-blind eyes
were seared to tears
as a silent blast blew their spirits free
of the chains of gravity, time, and space.
Our retinas, like magnifying glasses,
burned the after-image into our memories.

II: Memory

Jarvis, McAuliffe, McNair, Onizuka, Resnick, Scobee, Smith:
names that resonate in ripples,
a shock wave that radiates across boundaries
of geography and ideology:
Seven explorers stood at the edge of space
and dared the dragons of uncharted depths.
Male and female, oriental, black, and white,

they stood for us, and we stood with them
as they launched their names and atoms
into space-time and into history
and bequeathed to us their dreams.
Their smiles of confidence and courage
haunt the inner spaces of our memory.
Their names float like echoes in a dream
of the muted wail of a saxophone.
The images unite us in a web of memory
of seven stars that pass
from memory to myth.

III: Myth

Constellations in stately procession
swirl into configurations that spell
Orion, Hercules: man's images writ large
on the blank, black page of the universe.
But earthman, become starman,
has left his track on the moon,
pushed off to launch himself
into his own mythology,
to place himself among the star pictures
of his own heroes.
Seven stars rise in the east
to become a new constellation—
Icarus, the first man to reach beyond himself,
to shed the bonds of earth—
the failure of his melted wings
transmuted from tragedy to triumph
by the touchstone of mythology.
Courage, discipline, honor, intelligence,
curiosity, strength, sacrifice—

seven stars rise in the east,
giving us fixed points to steer by
in Einstein's universe of relativity.
Seven stars for Icarus,
Seven stars for mankind,
points to triangulate uncharted space,
they chart our outward path
from our fragile, blue-green cocoon
as our spirits follow their upward spiral
to the stars and to our last rendezvous
with destiny.

Enabling Ground

(For Seamus Heaney)

Against honeysuckled breeze of Southern spring
a brogue of Celtic poetry rolls.
The verses break in waves,
assault the vaulted rafters
of the academy.
The crash and flow of language
sweep listeners like vessels
to Ireland's emerald hills and stony ground,
to Belfast's barricaded streets,
to the stone tower of Thoor Ballylee,
to the Irish crowning place
of Tara's screaming stone,
and back, back to Beowulf's mead hall,
shaking with the songs of heroes' deeds.

The poet's ringing verse enchants.
He stands on modern ground;
with the ring of poetry
his voice evokes the bards,
the master spirits of each age.
They arise from ancient soil,
steeped in poetry and place
as the sacrificial victims
of Grauballe and Tollund
are preserved in the dark waters
of the eternal bogs.
They arise and add their chants
to the poems of Irish soil.
They stand their ground:
sounds and textures of their syllables
add to the geography of language,

the flowing streams of Gaelic
to the crags of gruff Germanic tongues.

Distant echoes blend
their ringing syllables,
assault the vaulted rafters
of mead halls and bardic haunts
beneath the gloomy shades
of druids' oaks.
Gaelic sacrificial chants
join Anglo-Saxon battlesongs,
hard-edged as swords on plated mail.

The Irish poet reads his verse
in academic halls.
Around him stand the wordsmiths, shades
who forged their ringing song
for stone-eyed men of battle
in a rough-beamed place of listening.
From academic auditorium to screaming stone,
from mead hall to druids' grove,
the poet's chanting voice creates,
recreates the land.
He stands at the place of making
at the source of inspiration,
at the sacramental site
of the enabling ground.

Fiat Lux

(For Virginia Spencer Carr)

I

As sunlight through stained glass illuminates,
its roseate glow igniting prayerful souls,
the teacher's wisdom, filtered through a smile,
enkindles smoldering sparks in glowing minds.
Effulgence of the intellect ignites,
by light and heat, the ember into flame.

Pure logic casts a cold fluorescent glare,
its focus, like a laser beam, dissects:
dispassionate analysis destroys
the beauty of the object scrutinized.
When thought is filtered through the human heart,
the beam diffracts to prism's bold array.

II

Her gracious southern smile testifies
to intellect infused with gentle warmth:
the teacher—master, guru, sensei, friend.
Soft voice reveals the rigors of research,
demands of academic discipline.

The facts and forms, discourse of scholarship,
convey more subtle truths to seeking minds.
The light and warmth of passion animates
cold facts, inspires wisdom in the soul.
As flame transmutes and purifies the dross,

emotion changes thought to purer being.

The course work finished, dissertation done,
the graduation hooding ritual,
the laying on of hands, through touch, confirms
the transformation: student into friend.

III

As beams of energy through time and space
project in waves across the universe,
from infrared to violet displayed,
Bright light, at once a rainbow radiance.
So thoughts, unchanged, eternal flow, combine.
Teacher and student, one in higher Mind.

The Return, an Elegy in Three Movements

I. Adagio

When life's abiding suffering relents
and passing pleasures dissipate like clouds,
the spasms of the heart release; the grasp
of passion eases; seeking mind is stilled.
As sound and colors unify and fail,
the spirit frees itself from clench of form.
The anima like wine from shattered cup
pours forth: the broken vessel stays behind,
its clay returns to elements of earth.
The crematory flame transmutes the flesh
to elements: air, water, earth, and fire.

II. Eroico con Maestoso

Atlantic: whispering blue expanse that calls
us back, the source, Dark Mother of us all.
Your restless waves cast up and then retrieve
the empty shells and ragged seaweed shreds
that mingle with the ebb and flow of sand.
Beyond the breakers' throb of rolling surf,
the multitudinous variety
of urgent lives flows on beneath your waves.
Like Brahma, Shiva, Vishnu all in one,
you give, preserve, and take the flow of life.
Your saline amniotic tide, that swirls
from plankton to the whales' majestic bulk,
gives life—and takes—with fang and grasping claw.
The pastel hues of flashing fins and scales
pursuing and pursued from life to life.
No ends and no beginnings: only flow
the forms and force of lives that interchange.

III. Appassionato

The yearning whisper of the ocean's waves
calls to the living at the water's edge,
reminder of their own mortality.
The lapping water sweeps the slipping sand
from under feet, of those who bid farewell.
The all-accepting sea in its embrace
enfolds the sift of ashes scattered forth,
reluctant hands release before the wind.
The mortal grit swirls down and disappears
beneath the ebbing foam, from death to life.
No end, but a beginning, subtle shifts
fulfilling forms of cosmic destinies.

IV. Coda

The flesh and spirit: separate and one,
disperse from form to formless, both transformed.
The one moves down, the other up and out.
The ashes swirl, becoming other beings,
the infinite taxonomies of life.
The luminescent life force dances free
to waltz upon the dark face of the deep.
It swirls with the slow and silent glide
of galaxies and nebulae that spin
beyond space-time, beyond the multi-verse.
Our life and death, the dance of energy
that flows in stately cadences of light,
attuned to silent symphonies of stars.

Cleaning Gutters

I stand at the top of the ladder
with my hands full of muck from the gutter;
the sun whispers through shining needles,
belying the winter solstice.
Brown leaves rattle in oak trees
next to slivers of evergreen,
shimmering the sibilant light with shades.
I stand on a rung under heaven,
mortality filling my hands.

In my hands are what leaves and needles become:
not the tender green of new growth
not the deceptive promise of midsummer health
when all life seems evergreen.
In my hands, with the mud, are the needles and leaves
of midsummer. The leaves are more substance than form,
the needles brittle and black
as the muck of which they become a part.

I stand at the top of the ladder
my dazzled eyes turned to the tops of the trees,
looking at high-hanging cones overhead,
which yield seed after their kind.
Winged seeds drop like tongues of flame,
bearing the message of life.
They descend like squadrons of angels;
their spiralling wings flash like swords.

My hands are full of the life-giving death
of needles and leaves.
Some seeds fall to the fertile ground,
while others fall to the roof

and blunt their points in the muck.
In the muck are the seeds of midsummer growth,
warmed by the sun of the solstice.

I stand at the top of the ladder,
mortality filling my hands.
In my hands are what leaves and needles become;
in the muck are the seeds of midsummer growth.
I stand on a rung between heaven and earth,
Immortality filling my hands.

Cruciverbalist

Black squares in abstract shapes,
a symmetry of form,
diagonals among the empty squares—
crossword puzzles, blank, await the pen:

Obscure linguistic trivia
(the proper names, abstruse geography,
and foreign words)
form enigmatic clues, across and down,
evoke the random patterns, a paradox
of language, connections
on a semiotic grid:
Language as signs, directing minds
to follow different paths of thought.

Clues elicit memories:
half-forgotten facts concealed
among the neurons, called up and locked
in perpendiculars.
Nouns, verbs, and adjectives unite
in unexpected schemes, not sentences,
but meanings change in the squares' geometry.

Linguistic chessboard challenges the mind.
One by one, the letters, pieces
in the endgame, snap in place,
The last vowel moves to check,
and the word game is fulfilled.

The pattern on the page that shifts
the meanings of the words

alters alike the network of the nerves:
the play of words
a seismic shift in
the brain's cartography.

SONNETS RENAISSANCE CONNECTIONS

Transcendent Aesthetic

The body, a disconsolate child, cries
and frets. Its constant unfulfilled desires
feed on themselves; slaked passions still arise
as wind incites the flame and fans the fire.
As shadows entertain the restless mind,
distractions flicker on the cave's dark wall:
bright lights and flashing colors, the design
enchants the senses, holding us enthralled.
The soul seeks comfort in philosophy:
as dogmas offer order and design.
The metaphysics of transcendency:
our thoughts and appetites transmute, refine.
As lotus blossoms rise from ooze below,
our essence lifts from feel and think to know.

A Father's Hands

His strong but gentle hands hold and protect
the child whose birth has changed his universe.
The tiny, throbbing heart his hands detect
echoes the pulse her parents' hearts rehearse.
She grasps his fingers in her tiny hands
to steady her first steps. His tender grip
provides the gentle power as she stands.
He hovers, hands prepared, if she should slip.
Throughout her life her father's hands are near
to shelter, to encourage, and to guide.
His reassuring hands allay her fears;
his touch conveys his sense of love and pride.
A father's hands protect a daughter's heart
And hold her love when they are far apart.

Ice Queen

Resplendent in the sable winter night,
she lies recumbent on a velvet bed.
Enticing and aloof, her charms delight
and thwart her desperate lovers who are led
by silver light through shadowed dreams of bliss.
She draws them on, enchanted by her arts
of necromancy, to the dark abyss.
They offer up the shards of shattered hearts,
but she ignores their ardent sacrifice.
Surrounded by her frigid crystal orb,
reserved behind a pristine ring of ice,
she does not let their distant cries disturb
her equanimity. She floats above,
indifferent to the fervent plaints of love.

Katharsis

When passions overrun the poet's heart,
assailing his defenses with their bolts
and wreaking havoc with their flaming darts,
the poet takes his pen to quell revolts
inciting insurrections in the blood.
The sonnet builds a rigid wall of lines
that shapes the feelings' else-chaotic flood.
Emotions, channeled by the strict designs
of meter and of rhyme scheme, lose their might.
As demons, named, are conjured to obey
the sorcerer whose spells put them to flight
like evening mists before the light of day:
  so passion's haunting spirits must disperse
  before the poet's weaving wand of verse.

Mistress/Muse

Her gentle whisper wakens me from sleep.
She summons me, submerged in silent dreams.
My consciousness ascends from fathoms deep,
arising through emotions' swirling streams.
Her touch arouses me, my blood tide crests
and flows in waves of passion to my brain.
The pulse that pounds within my beating breast
sweeps onward, carries me to pleasure's pain.
I rise, responding to her potent urge
to satisfy desires that elate,
swept, helpless, by desire's desperate surge,
submitting to the passion to create.
The sleepless poet, helpless to refuse,
gives in to the insistence of the muse.

Prince of Fools

A fortress built of granite looms above
as I prepare my sword for the assault.
Knight errant, riding forth in search of love,
I search the walls for any flaw or fault.
With feather-crested helmet, visor down,
I wait for my opponent to appear.
My challenger appears with princess' crown,
her lovely face confirming my worst fear.
Her scornful laugh turns helm to cap and bells;
my burnished sword becomes a paper knife.
My courage fails before her potent spell
that withers passion at the source of life.
  Behind the walls of apathy she rules:
  the Knight of Love becomes the Prince of Fools.

Bewitched

Dark eyes, which gleam and promise greater heat
of love, cast secret spells with midnight glance:
a look, at once impassioned and discreet,
designed to captivate, enthrall, entrance.
Full lips, which smile and whisper quiet words,
invoke a spirit with enchanter's art.
A charm, perhaps implied, perhaps inferred,
entices and bewitches heedless hearts.
Behind the eyes and lips a Presence waits
for signs of love to shine in others' eyes.
The Goddess from whose soul love emanates
looks on and smiles, beneficent and wise.
The spell of love that flickers in her face
bestows on human hearts divinest grace.

Potentiality

The open petals of a pouting rose
exude a sweet, intoxicating scent.
As petals open, so the fragrance grows:
a whisper in the air, a subtle hint,
becomes a shout of perfume in the air.
The blushing petals spread before the gaze
of eyes amazed by beauty, lush and fair,
until its freshness withers and decays.
The undeveloped bud, more self-possessed,
withholds its beauty from the careless glance.
Its scent more subtle than full openness,
more likely to entice than to entrance.
 Anticipation sharpens appetite:
 potential pleasure doubles the delight.

Spirits
(A Sonnet Sequence)

I. Spirits Past

As Socrates stood in the noise and heat
Of Athens' crowded marketplace, he saw
A world abstract behind the world concrete,
A world controlled by universal law.
Pythagoras and Euclid, with their rules
And compasses, found a cosmology
Governed by numbers, measured by their tools.
Philosophers, whose eyes have learned to see
Beyond the chaos of a tumbling world,
Have spoken to us down through every age,
Their wisdom like a banner held unfurled
To lead us in the battle that we wage.
Their voice a clarion call, they lead the fight
Against the foes of order, truth, and right.

II. Spirits Present

We stand before our students every day,
Reciting facts and teaching concrete skills.
Behind those facts, the subjects we convey,
A deeper purpose lies. The truth fulfills
Itself with every syllable we speak.
A wisdom beyond facts becomes our end,
As truth becomes the chalice that we seek.
Our students are the envoys that we send
To search for meaning, carrying the quest
Beyond our classrooms. Their ears now attend
To whispers of those spirits who invest

Them with the search for education's end.
The voices send them forth, in all their youth,
To carry on the quest for higher truth.

III. Spirits Future

They stand before the soft, enchanting song
Of pleasures and possessions. Each bright sound
Entices them: the call is sweet and strong
And weaves a web that holds them all spellbound.
But, trumpet-clear, the voices of the past
Recall them from the rocks to which they're led.
The voice of truth maintains their course steadfast
And guides them back to safer paths instead.
Pythagoras and Plato stand behind
Our thoughts, their whispered voices never still.
Their works convey a sense of larger Mind
And of a larger order to fulfill.
Through centuries, their whispers to the soul
Remind us all of our still-distant goal.

Phoenix

"The soul of man is a flame: a bird of fire "
Nikos Kazantzakis, "The Saviors of God"

By what instinct, by what sure memory
Are you moved? Who taught you the ageless art?
Whence the instinct of immortality?
When, somewhere in your soul, you feel the spark
Of an idea, you construct your pyre-nest,
Scented with spikenard, frankincense, and myrrh.
Upon the scented pile you take your rest,
And crimson wings fan crimson flames that stir
And blaze like leaping plumes of fire. The heat
Intensifies, becomes a furnace blast;
The fragrant flame of death your life completes,
Creates life from the ashes of the past.
Purified, you step forth newly wrought,
Self-immolated and thus self-begot.

Re: Cycles

(For the Class of 2011)
"In my end is my beginning."
–T. S. Eliot

The endings and beginnings of our lives
define us as we seek our destiny.
Our upward spiral shapes us as we strive:
the sweep of cycles shapes our harmony.
A circle from a central point begins,
concluding where it starts, a unity.
The Alpha and Omega joined, it spins:
the compass circumscribes eternity.
The circles of our lives thus intertwine.
We graduate to larger destinies.
Our cycles with the universe align–
majestic sweep of spinning galaxies.
Around a central point, our arc ascends,
One cycle starts, here, where another ends.

HAIKU
ASIAN
CONNECTIONS

Butterfly

A butterfly lands
On a rose petal, mingles
Pollen and wing dust.

Water

Mist, ice, and water:
Powerful, passive, it flows—
Limitless as life.

Tree on Lu Mountain

Sculpted by the wind,
Bowing, clings to craggy cliff:
Nature's Bonsai art.

Meditation

Heart beat in silence,
Whispering a syllable:
Voiceless voice of breath.

Caterpillar

Caterpillar crawls,
Eats, spins its cocoon, and sleeps:
Dreams of wings and flight.

Memory

Full moon reflected,
The lake serene, clear, and calm:
A leaf falls—ripples!

Autumn Haiku

Orion rising
Over rustling autumn leaves:
Lonely cricket chirps.

Running Haiku

Mercury's winged heels:
Like lightning, racing feet flash:
Dreams of running shoes.

Cherry Trees

A breeze: pink cloud drifts.
Petals fall, a pastel rain—
Not tree, but mind shifts.

Bamboo Flute

Bamboo flute recalls
Breeze through leaves–each note:
Whispered memory.

Hershey's Kiss: a Haiku

Silver volcano:
melting—chocolate lava flow—
liquid lusciousness.

THE WEB OF

INDRA

At the Reading

On a break from reading essays,
I bask, face turned toward the sun,
seeking serenity and warmth from its illumination.
Beyond the hotel, the beach of Daytona:
the waves of the Atlantic whisper
their secrets—
the rhythmic wordless word.

Pelicans glide overhead,
stately in formations that flow
and change, their choreography wind-wafted:
an avian ballet.
In water or on earth,
their odd anatomy and unlikely beak
(though a triumph of evolution)
amuse more than inspire.
Aloft, that odd ungainliness
transforms itself to grace.
I watch a moment more
before returning to my task.

The adolescent essays that I read
(full of earnest energy
and passionate belief)
aspire to uplift, to illuminate.
They struggle against gravity.
Like pelicans on wings of words,
they rise.

The patterns of their thoughts,
their choreography, transforms
the whisper of their thoughts
To words.

They rise, in-spired by the wind
of breath,
to flow, transformed,
from ungainliness to grace.

Adversity

A room, full of readers, silent,
but for the whisper of pages.
Like meditating monks, we bow
and score the papers placed before us.
The adolescent angst flows
across the page
in rivers of ink (or blood).
They pour the contents (and discontents)
of hearts and souls
upon the page before us,
as we sit in judgment
of their proffered offerings.
Life is suffering indeed.
If essays were not soundless,
the room, as silent as a meditation hall,
would echo with the writers' voices.
The moans and sobs, the gasps
would drift like smoke across the room.
A haze of feelings hovers
over humbled heads.
We bow before their pathos
as we meditate upon
our own adversity.

Aquarians

In the silver sweep of the moonlight,
we sit on the cold, damp sand.
Our whispers are muted by the sigh
of exhausted waves
as they fling themselves
toward the shore.
Overhead, in stately choreography,
Orion, Virgo, and Sagittarius promenade
to the silent song of the cosmos.
The Water-Bearer pours forth an ocean of stars
from his overturned vessel
to fill the night sky with dancing lights.

We sit and watch on the sand below.
Our blood tide echoes the heave
of the waves
as our minds reel with the stars.

Fruit Fullness

Sunbeams enfold the gold and crimson curve
of fragrant flesh and warm the velvet blush
to deeper hue. Sweet succulence flows forth
in rivulets from bruise of gentle bite.

The ripeness burst its nectar on the tongue
and yields its sweetness to the gentle probe
that plunges to the center's deeper red
and finds fulfillment in the waiting seed.

Ash Wednesday Service

The silver-crescent chalice rim cradles the Eastern
like an ancient mysterious icon held aloft
by stark, black limbs
against the purple sky.
The church is solemn-silent.
The stained glass color,
deepened by the night,
withstand the press
of darkness that contends
with flickering candle flames.
Isaiah's bleak admonitions
reverberate over brooding heads,
bent on forgiveness.
Our foreheads bear the smudge
of our mortality.
The circle of innocent bread glows
above the gold-gleam of the cup,
raised by consecrated hands.
Chastised, we kneel repentant
of our prodigality,
but wrapped in consolation
by the ransomed sacrifice.
No longer Cain-marked, cursed
by sin, we are sealed
against the dark.
As we leave, the light
from open doors cascades
down darkened steps.
The diamond-spangled velvet sky backdrops a silver-sliver moon.

Necropolis
(Oakland Cemetery)

The city of the dead
reposes beneath a pall of clouds.
Subdivisions are laid out
in geometric forms,
delineated by a gridwork of paths
named for the long-dead.
Square plots, subdivided
into rectangular graves,
serve as last addresses for the dead.

Haughty mausoleums, marble mansions,
stand in weighty, supercilious grace:
superior even in death,
the rich dissolve to dust
in whited tombs
above the weathered, stone-marked graves.
In potter's field the homeless dead,
anonymous in death as life,
repose forgotten underneath
their waving monuments of grass.

The statuary monuments—
of risen Christs, of resting lambs,
and trumpeting Gabriels—
rise hopefully toward cloud-closed skies.
And on the stones, inscriptions bear
their witness to the hopes and griefs
of those still living, left behind.

But those who lie beneath the marble slabs
or save their bones in granite vaults

lie oblivious in their last sleep,
unaware of marble monuments
with hopeful epitaphs,
unaware of the plotted geometry
of the molds of death.
Outside human space and time,
they sleep in the continuum
of the long instant of eternity.

(K)armadillo

In an attitude of surrender,
legs jutting to the sky,
it lies by the side of the road.
Like an alien creature lost
in space and time,
the Texas state mammal has traveled
to die on Georgia clay.
What impulse in its tiny brain
compelled its pilgrimage?
What archetypal armadillo quest
finds its fulfillment here?

Its nine bands of armor, bony plates
like medieval mail,
seem a Jurassic throwback,
a cosmic joke to prove
(or disprove) evolution's truth.

The armadillo (defenses ineffectual
against the automobile)
fulfills its destiny,
its decomposing stench
a dinner call to seething swarms
of insects that, in life,
had been its prey.

Its life—and death—a mystery,
the armadillo devolves into
its primal elements:
the proof (perhaps) of larger cosmic truths—
or comic irony.

From His Coy Mistress

Had you but words enough and rime,
I might give your proposal time.
I'd listen to what you have to say,
Amused by your witty words' display.
I'd lie by whate'er stream you asked,
While you in my attention basked.
I'd listen to your verbal flood,
The torrent of your passion's blood,
Considering each point you choose
To convince or to amuse.
Your catalog of body parts
Serves to display your verbal arts:
Professions of your sweet desire
To kindle in my heart a fire.
You're right, that time's in swift pursuit;
That argument I'll not refute.
The tomb awaits my mortal dust
If I deny your burning lust.
My flesh may be the food of worms,
As you explain in graphic terms.
The grave's, indeed, a private bed,
But not one whose embrace I dread.
Therefore, though my life's youthful blush
Comes to my face in sanguine rush,
My soul's eternal youth conspires
Against the act your lust requires.
Though time devours my mortal flesh,
My spirit lives, untouched and fresh.
My body passes iron gates:
My soul avoids that mortal fate.
Your arguments, with wit and grace,

Entice me to your warm embrace.
But clever rimes and witty words
Fall on my ears and die, unheard.
Though Marvell with your words you be,
Your clever lines are lost on me.

Quentin

Adrift upon the stream of consciousness,
the swirl and eddies of the tide of time,
I flounder in the currents of my life
and love. The shadows, like a spectral hand,
point an accusing finger toward my death.

My sister: mother, lover, shifting masks
of archetypal women in your face:
you haunt my days and dreams. The siren song
calls up from murky depths, entices me
to heart's desire, and soul's eternal loss.
I plunge to depths of darkness to escape
the tick of time. My love and passion flow.
The whirl and churn unite us in their dance.

Two people, drowning, desperate, cling to life:
each other's hope, become each other's doom.
Releasing you, I plunge lonely depths
while gasping for the kiss that steals your breath.

Forbidden knowledge, Tree that cannot save:
the fruit whose bitter aftertaste is death.
The branches that I clutch refuse my grip,
releasing me to slip beneath the waves.
The swirling moils of the current, time,
seduce me to the timelessness of death.

The Dance of Creativity

The Yin and Yang of creativity
engage the dance of life, the complex gift
of art and intellectuality:

the thought and feeling in duality,
a stately waltz of elements that shift,
the constant flux of circularity.

Einstein and Mozart's choreography,
the cosmic dance, as minds and hearts uplift,
enlarges visions of reality.

Though Torrance quantifies ability,
the measure of the dance is not the gift:
as numbers hobble art's agility

and freezes movement, chills intensity.
The mind an heart, unfettered, spin and drift;
but measured, lose the dance of harmony.

Though we may watch the dance, diversity
must dance unhampered, following its gift,
the art of intellectuality—
eternal Tao of creativity.

Honeysuckle and Wisteria

The fragrance lazes out
a tendril of sweetness
to caress the unsuspecting passerby.
Wisteria and honeysuckle of the southern spring
swell and exude.

Wisteria blooms drip in bunches
like fragrant purple grapes,
swollen and ripe;
the wine of their heavy blossoms intoxicates
as it twines around and captivates.

Honeysuckle (its name so evocative)
opens mellifluous petals,
pouting, drooping golden,
dripping honeyed fragrance
to confuse enchanted bees.

Honeysuckle and wisteria—
the one delicate in bridal pastels
of yellow and white;
the other gauded out in purple sensuality—
honey and wine entice,
intoxicate, entrance.
And while the fragrances exude,
a soft perfume from pouting lips,
the vines extend their touch
to cling, embrace, and choke.

Turning Forty

The day dawned with no black edges,
like an obituary page.
The sun still gilded morning clouds
and brightened autumn's palette
on late September leaves.

I woke and watched the sun illuminate
the curved edge of the turning world.
I listened for the tick
of turning galaxies
measuring the moments of eternity.

I heard, instead, the mockingbirds
burst forth in complicated urgency
their celebrated, sweet aubade
of harmonic jubilation.

A year closer to glory,
a step closer to wisdom,
I watch the decades turn
like leaves
and celebrate in song
a passing golden moment
of eternity.

Freudian Slips: April Fools

Through the drowsy April afternoon
the learned lecture rattles
like oak leaves on a winter branch.
Over somnolent adolescent heads
the voice drones on
through vaguely Teutonic catalogues
of complexes and neuroses
and dream interpretations.

Outside the window, early bees slip inside
       the blush
of pristine cherry petals.
They buzz
       among the blossoms,
their unrequited lust
          for nectar
satisfying the flowers' deeper need
to pollinate the waiting seed
       and procreate their kind.

In the classroom, students, mesmerized,
       slip into unconscious reveries.
Their heartbeats pound, reverberating
       Stravinskian percussion,
blood rhythms throb and overwhelm
       the academic hum.
Their dreams, unanalyzed and un-interpreted,
       drift
          like pollen
through their fertile minds.
       Their instinct to pleasure dominates
the sterile intellect;

the forces of life
flit
from blossom
to blossom,
less interested in concepts
than conception.

Hedging Bets

Straight lines and planes–Aren't nature's form:
She does her Work–in curves.
She doesn't follow Euclid's laws;
A subtler Theorem serves.

The Hedges grow–in fits and starts,
Destroying careful Planes,
Right angles ruined–by careless leaves
That Pruning can't restrain.

Through suburban–Summer days
I try my level best,
Squaring off–against the Growth
That Sprouts back as I rest.

The hedge is Wrenched–to Human lines
By humming pruner blades;
And nature's Force–seems held in check,
Man's Dominance displayed.

The planes are smooth,–the Angles sharp
As by Surveyor's chain,
Denying Mutability
And hedges seem–Restrained.

But Nature continues as I stop
to sight down–measured edge.
I know my Work's futility
Against–the sprouting hedge.

Man's Thoughts and tools–enforce the Forms
As He molds Nature's lines;
Until She prunes Him–like the hedge
To fit Her own Design.

Kinder, Gentler

He lurches down heaving sidewalks,
brain reeling from the fumes
of alcohol and the inhaled vapors
of Lysol spray.
Invisible behind labels—
the conservative "wino" and "bum"
or the neo-liberal "homeless"—
his red eyes glare
from behind hair and dirt
as he curses a deaf world.
A trash bag full of beer cans
slung on his back,
a nightmare Santa Claus,
he descends on a beer can
someone has killed.
The trickle-down evaporates
before it reaches him,
except for the trickle
of warm, flat beer
from a crushed, discarded can.
Continuing his unsteady work,
he rolls down wobbly sidewalks,
a staggering statistic.
He floats toward a handout
and a half pint
of oblivion,
with no job, no responsibility,
and no hope.

Le Petit Mort

Shuddering–
       Possessing and possessed
              by one another–
         and by the deeper need
imbedded in the helix strands:
         a procreative spasm
acknowledging and resisting the darkness.

Impulses spark across the nerves,
          non-being flashes into being.

Eros and Thanatos,
     From darkness, we fumble
toward the light,
         a flash among the shadows
like lightning across the clouds
     at night.

The new-begotten are charged
          with our energy
across the circuits
 generated and regenerated.

As our spark dissolves to darkness,
     the afterimage of our flash
is translated into flesh
     as we live on in the afterglow
of life.

The Least of These
(For Carl Bohannon)

He lies outstretched on new-washed sheets,
his pale, exhausted flesh spiked
by I-V needles.
Large hands, now soft,
surrender to their forced repose,
resigned to the indignities
of age.

Stripped and robed in a borrowed gown, he lies,
his loins girt in humiliating cloths
against the unchecked functions
of corrupt mortality.
Meekly he accedes to the needles and the pills,
the proddings of starched angels
who invade his privacy.
Hands offer him a paper cup.
He drains the bitter draught
and gags.
The frailties of his exhausted age
resist the potions and technology
of the healers' helpless arts.

A glimmer lurks behind his restless eyes,
a candle flame that flickers.
His fragile smile flashes
the innocence of age,
the Alpha and Omega
of human life.

He suffers in stoic silence,
awaiting his reprieve from pain.
His willing spirit hangs
upon a cross of failing flesh,
as he awaits redemption
from his life.

In Memoriam Juvenum

(For Jennifer Duffala, Pam Kim,
Jonathan Price, and Jacque Suter)

The polished mahogany gleams,
the grain illumined
by a deep, subtle glow,
as though the wood recalls
the vital heat of sunlight
deep within its cells.
The riveted plate of burnished bronze,
counterpoints the gentle warmth of wood.

The simple dignity
of the letters of a name,
inscribed in hard-edged letters,
remind us of our loss.
The dates of birth and death signify
the beginning and the end
of life.

Names and dates engraved in plaques
cannot contain the meaning of a life
or convey the anguish of a life
cut short.
The agonies of heart-hurt,
burned deep in memory,
endure beyond inscriptions
cut in metal plates or carved in stone.
The vital heat of memories
abides within the soul
and emanates a flame that fuels itself.

Though wood-and-metal plaques remind us
of the stark realities of birth and death,
the heart alone preserves
the constant fire of memory
and the meaning of a life.

Processional

Communicants tread their cautious ways
through frozen slush of winter dawn.
Downturned eyes peer from shaded depths,
contemplative beneath scarves and hats.
Their frosted breath plumes out
like fragrant censer smoke.
The wind whips unprotected skin
and scatters snow
like ashes on their heads.

Toward offices in halls of gold
they move. Their solemn pace is measured,
their matins plainsong answered
by the polyphonic horns'
antiphonal response.
In passing buses, row on row
of nodding supplicants
devote themselves
to Wall Street's beatific text.
Converging on their cells
in halls of trade,
the acolytes proceed
through dim-lit, dirty streets.

Unseen by downturned eyes,
the eastern skyline glows, flecked
with dawn-dappled tangerine clouds.
Overhead, the violet sky
flaunts a fading crescent moon
and one bright star.

Reunion

Time twists and turns
on itself like a mobius strip
to become the emblem
of eternity.
A line, once drawn,
continues
through all the undulations
until the ends unite.
Within the curve of space and time
two points on a line evolve:
the further apart they separate,
the closer to reunion.

Through all the convolutions
of a life,
a relationship revolves, involves.
Through Eternal Recurrence
we separate to reunite.
We flow through changes
and exchanges
until we get it
right.

Re Vision

Vision

In wooden ships with wing-white sails
they plowed the gray Atlantic waves.
Daring the rolling pastures
of un-Jonahed whales,
they set their eyes on New Jerusalem.
Louder than wind-roar and lightning crack
of the North Atlantic rage
their ears rang with the Word
of King James' Old-Testament Jehovah.
With their feet set
on foam-flecked Plymouth Rock
and the rising sun at their backs,
they cast long shadows across the land.

From stone-walled, narrow city streets
and thatch-roofed huts,
undaunted by the dense-treed wilderness,
came iron men and women.
They plowed the fertile earth
with steel-tipped ploughshares
and brought forth upon the land
their vision of the promised life.

In canvas-sheeted Conestogas
they crossed the rolling continent.
The jolting buckboards rattled teeth
and jarred bones
as wagon trains serpentined
across the Great Plains
and looped, tortuous, through the Rockies.

Their hard eyes squinted level
against the setting sun.

The villages they planted,
as they crossed the virgin land,
sprouted and grew to cities,
taller than the redwoods
against the horizon's blue immensity.
The vision of the New World
gleamed golden, beacon-bright.

Blindness

The cities grew
and spread.
Smoke stacks sprang like toadstools
and spouted clouds of brimstone smoke.
Once sparkling rivers slowed
to sludge.
The fertile soil yielded up its life
to pavement and pollution.
The Promised Land was bartered,
auctioned bit by bit,
sectioned off by gleaming rails,
and tortured to submission
by boundaries of barbed wire.
The vision of America
became clouded
and distorted
by the near-sightedness
of myopic materialism.

Re Vision

But the sun still blazes bright
above the yellow clouds.
The rivers, from their fountainheads
spring sparkle-fresh,
and Earth, in all her deep fertility,
still feeds the world made fresh
with the light of every rising sun.

The iridescent arc extends
between two oceans,
a spectrum of the covenant of hope.
And downturned eyes,
though clouded by the mote
of pleasure and pollution,
can still gaze upward
like the eagles' eyes.
The sun still casts a rainbow
in the clouds,
a promise, a re vision
of the dream.

Vacancy

Apartment windows, stripped
of drapes, stare like dilated eyes.
Behind them, empty rooms
seem now so large
and small.
The contents of a life,
packed for departure,
leave, not just space
but a void.
Conversations switch to past
and future, tense
at the last poised moment.
The door, closed a last time,
echoes in the emptiness.
Last tearful hugs and smiles—
a joy akin to grief
fills the parting
with something like relief.
The tail lights blink a final sign
as eyes blink back the tears
and turn to face
the vacancy.

Winter Night

Moonlight is cold comfort
on such a night.
Hard-edged stars blink
against the dark,
like Christmas-tree lights;
their fires do not warm.
The shoveled paths, worn
by booted feet,
have frozen into ruts.
A snowman stands,
lone sentry of a bleak expanse
of blue-white snow:
his open arms and stony smile
offer frigid solace to the passerby.
Ice-glazed branches, their buds
clenched against the cold,
rattle in the wind.
Dark shadows of trees and snowman
stretch across the rutted snow.
The passerby hurries back
to lighted windows
and the warmth of fireside.
Moonlight is cold comfort
on such a silent night.

Chiron

Brute-bodied flesh below
and human form above:
while, upward, my mind strains to soar,
downward, hoof clops
drag in mortal dust:
Granted immortality but denied divinity;
Mentor of the gods,
but refused an Olympian throne.
My fingers fondle lyre strings,
enticing gentle strains.
Apollo plucks my nerves;
reverberating harmonic notes
shimmer down my bones.
But my beast heart pounds percussion,
blood gallops down the muscle humps
and throbs through massive limbs.

Through verdant Arcadian forests
and sun-dappled bowers, I race
with the virgin Diana.
Past piping fauns and wood nymphs,
sporting in innocent lust,
we race—she riding, I running, slung-bellied—
hunting the rutting stag.
Her chaste beauty slashes my eyes,
flashes across my soul
like lightning across dark night.
But behind my adoration burns
my stallion lechery.
Her tempting female flesh exudes
tendrils of musky scent
that tease me to tumescence.

The blood tide swells in muscles
that thrill to music's beat.
My clumsy hooves but stumble
to music's gentle dance;
my visions of perfect beauty
are warped by clouds of lust.
The animal I drag behind
attaches me to earth.

Upward a god, downward a beast,
I contradict myself.
But though my horsey body
disgusts my human soul
with its lustful, gross desires,
I revel in the lava tides
that pound through throbbing veins.

Without those fiery passions
that rage with wild heat,
my soul would chill from frigid touch
of icy intellect.
Though denied Olympus' lofty view,
I feel earth's vital flame:
the passions of my animal—
my glory and my shame.

Butterfly

The butterfly flits on the dancing breeze
through summer's golden hour.
She flicks her fragile fairy wings
and dances with each bright flower.

The flowers welcome her tender touch
and open seductive petals.
She tastes in turn their sweet delights—
she sips but never settles.

Throughout the days of summer's warmth
she dallies in nectared bliss.
Each flower dances to her touch
and bends before her kiss.

But flowers wilt before the wind
of autumn's bitter cold.
The petals fade to withered brown
that once had glistened gold.

The butterfly, tossed before the blast,
her days of leisure flown,
seeks in vain a refuge,
unsheltered and alone.

Memento Vitae
(For Bill Thomas)

The ancient hero, fallen brave in battle,
gathered wealth and fame before his death.
Gold giver, loved by family and friends,
was honored in the glory of his life.
In death, his gleaming armor filled the barge
that launched his soaring spirit on the sea.
Set free from worldly bonds, his valiant soul
in victory arose to its reward,
the treasures of his life gold-gleaming,
as he ascended to Valhalla's gates.

So we commit your body to the waves,
launched forth upon the waters and the wind.
Brave in battle, facing bitter pain,
you fought with quiet strength, your valiant soul
unbowed and undefeated, facing death.
Now, honored in the glory of your life,
surrounded by your family and friends,
you take a wealth of love, its golden gleam
the treasure of your life as you ascend
to heaven's bright reward beyond the stars.
And we, who loved and honored you in life,
launch you to sail death's bright, uncharted seas.
Your harbor is assured, the beacon burns
to guide you to God's sheltered golden shores.

(Im)Permanence
(An Elegy)

The lake beneath the late-October sky
reflects gray clouds, adrift on drift
of wind-waft waves that whisper to the rocks.
The shared communion-wake of family
and friends: we shiver on the dock; the leaves
that rustle on the half-stripped oaks
remind us of our own mortality.
We pause, with drinks in hand, acknowledging
the moment of a passing; one by one,
our memories and tributes are cast forth
like pastel petals, pressed and dried:
the subtle fragrance of the ebbing past.

Processional of ashes carried forth,
she bears her love and grief in trembling hands:
small measure of a life, a simple urn.
A moment in eternity arrives.
We stand, backs to the wind, with tousled hair:
at wavering attention, voices hushed.
The whispered prayers of water and the wind
make requiems redundant: wordless words.

The ashes, gray on gray, across the clouds,
reflected in the somber swell of waves.
Her fingers stretch, caress the mortal grit,
both holding and releasing life and love.
The unsubstantial powder wafts to wind,
swirls to disappear from human sight.
The elements, combined, create a life:
dispersed become quintessences of dust.

We trudge back up the hill, our farewells done,
recite the platitudes of grief and loss:
The hugs and reassurances we share
directed both to others and ourselves.
We each emerge into the autumn air
and hear once more the whisper of the leaves.
As we resume our lives, the engines start.
The headlights pierce the dusk,
as each departs into the coming dark.

Puppet Dreams

After the performance,
lumber animated by a web
of dreams
in children's eyes,
for whom no distinction between is and seems,
who fill in truth for lies.
After the performance,
threads of destiny
are neatly wrapped,
and folded limbs returned
to dark confines of wooden walls.
Inappropriate,
the faces frozen into smiles, frowns,
applause falls on wooden ears.
After the performance,
wide-eyed dreams of children,
come wide-eyed dreams
of marionettes.
what figures flash behind the painted eyes?
Dreams of the stage?
Of Cinderella, Hamlet?
Of gilt-and-glitter costumes,
befitting noble gestures?
Or playing before kings?
Or dreaming, like Pinnochio
Of freedom from their strings?

Behind the blank, insensate eyes,
visions of sunlight-dappled hills;
behind the carved and painted ears
echoes of robin's morning song.

Shaped limbs tremble in memory
of wind-strings tugging leafy limbs.

After the performance,
and the spurious, stringed existence
of the stage;
after the empty gestures
and the tyranny of strings and script
and the fluttering echo of applause;
after the halting, submissive bows are made;
after the performance,
and the stringed, spasmodic dance,
the puppet dreams
alone, in a darkened wooden box,
not of is, but seems.

Rainbow Moment

Driving into afternoon sun
And into sudden cloud burst—
My sunglasses and wipers were useless:
The elements conspired to blindness.

Then I turned aside and stopped
To see the rainbow that I knew
Would be there among the clouds—it was:
The elements inspired to enlightenment.

Pommes

Taut globes of fragrant flesh,
that tempt the eyes, the tongue,
droop pendulous on branches.
The sanguine red, the verdant greens,
the blushing pink
of sweet varieties of apples.

At once a common fruit
and seductive archetype,
the fruit became a fatal flaw:
 Eris's Olympian revenge,
Eve's Edenic downfall,
Atalanta's gold seduction.
Prolific fruits, gold-gleaming, entice
in Botticelli's Spring,
with the promise of sweet fecundity.

Their shapes and hues and textures
seduce, alike the painter's eye.
Cezanne still lifes,
(impressions from a palette
of pastel shades and aureate tones
like brush strokes dipped in sunlight)
allure the palate and the eye.
Honeyed yellows, tart greens, intoxicating reds:
piquant pigments tantalize.
Surfeit of shapes and images fulfill
and satiate the mind.

Malus Domestica, from wild Asian orchards

to western cultivars:
from simple fruit to symbol,
from sweet delight to icon,
the apple fills my senses,
the apple of my mind.

In the Recital Hall

(for David Bottoms)

The poet stands on stage and reads
verses that recall, reshape his memories
in measured lines and metaphors,
remembrances of his father
from vibrant male to frail old age.

We sit in semi-darkness
as the poet, illumined by the stage lights,
shares his father's slow descent
into dim forests of dementia,
pursued and lost.

But as the shadows crowd around us in the hall,
a trumpet from a distant practice room
punctuates each line
and fills each pause with light.
The golden notes from scales,
honey-toned melody,
breaks through the dark
like sunlight dapples forest gloom.

The last poem read,
the poet's voice is still,
as sound dissipates to silence.
A trumpet note, like Gabriel's decrescendo,
whispers through the air,
an overtone to our applause.
It fades as house lights rise,
forestalling the unilluminated gloom
of our mortality.

LOVE KNOTS

Tantric Knowledge

He went in unto her, and he knew her,
And she conceived.

What do we learn
When we approach and open
To another?
Do we read the body's braille:
The textures, shapes, and qualities
Of muscle, skin, and bone?
Do we pulse with the rhythms
Of the heart and lungs,
Sympathetic harmonic vibrations
That echo back our own?

Beneath the topography of flesh
What knowledge lurks and waits?
How do we conceive the soul
That flows beneath the thrust
And flutter of the flesh?
Do our hearts open like petals
Before the probing butterfly?

Do we take on the knowledge
And conceive divinity, as god and goddess
(the knower and the known)
In tantric union intertwine?
In the Communion of the soul and flesh,
The opposites of yin and yang:
Do two become the One?

Helen among the Trojans

Her laughter chimes and charms down corridors
like Aphrodite's silver temple bells,
enchanting notes that echo down the halls
of Priam's royal palace. Troy's great pride
and shame, the prize of Paris' foolish choice,
fair Helen strums my heart like lyre strings.
A blind man's dormant passions, long forgot,
are resurrected, like the dragon crew
that Jason faced. Her fragrance haunts my dreams:
the wafting, silken scents of sandalwood
and frankincense still linger in my mind
when she has passed before my sightless gaze.
The songs I sing of ringing deeds of war
are silenced by the whisper of her walk.

Beyond the barrier of Trojan walls,
the clash of mortal battle fills the air.
Akahaian warriors, bearing brazen arms,
assail the city; screams rise from the throats
of dying men, impaled on blood-slaked swords.
their screams are echoed by the anguished moans
of wives embracing gore-encrusted forms.
The iron stench of blood drifts through the night.
The dark air reeks with smoke from flaming pyres;
the redolence of flesh provokes my thoughts
with bloody thoughts of war: of crimson mist,
of silhouetted figures waging war,
like shades from Hades, men already dead;
the men whose mortal screams split daylight air,
whose blazing bonfires dot the darkened plain,
disturb my dreams with images of death.

But still, within the unbreached walls of Troy,
King Priam sits in silence on his throne
while Hektor shouts and postures in the halls.
Kassandra speaks unheeded prophecies
of treachery and bloody deeds of war,
and women curse fair Helen's flawless face
because she brought Akhaian battleships
across the wine-dark sea to Trojan shores.
Through all the chaos of impending doom,
I hear her still, her voice a melody
above the clash of war's cacophony.
The spicy fragrance of her sweet perfume
entwines with acrid, pungent pyre smoke.
The sounds and smells of love and death, thus joined,
create a counterpoint within my heart.
Beyond the acts, alike, of war and love,
I sit within, my darkness and my age
deny the deeds of men which I might do.
My fingers fondle strings. My aging heart
remembers passions' rhythms in its beat,
and Helen's beauty haunts my sightless dreams.

Elemental Communion

An Epithalamion

As sun and rain, with earth and air, unite
To quicken and transform to grain and grape:
The terra cotta shades of earth distill
To regal hues of violet and gold.
Then, leavened and fermented, each transmutes
Quintessences of spirit out of earth.
Thus, wine and bread, communion's outward signs,
Transcend their humble elemental source.

Like bread and wine, a man and woman join,
Their separate elements by love combined,
Their union a communion: grain and grape
Distilled by spirit to a purer form.
As blush of grape is quickened into wine,
And grain engendered into living bread,
So man and woman, charged by passion's spark,
Become one flame, a purifying blaze
Amalgamating two souls into one.

Two sacramental unions, joined by love,
As man and woman, bread and wine evoke,
Completing, each the other, flesh and soul:
Communion of the essences of life.

Communion at Cana

A Wedding Poem

Quickening

Nestled by the Sea of Galilee,
the town of Cana, like a diadem
embedded on a brilliant tapestry,
lies still among the fields of infant green.
On olive trees the tender budding leaves
the harbingers of summer's fertile fruit,
embrace the sunlight's vital, warming touch.
As tendrils grope like fingers toward the light,
from deep beneath the parched expanse of earth
cool water rises, flows to roots that swell
to round the fragile grapes with bursting juice.

Union

From Cana's narrow, dusty streets arise
the joyful, ringing strains of wedding songs.
The solemn vows are said, the cup is crushed,
the feast is spread before the wedding guests
who raise their simple cups in joyful toasts
before the blushing bride and cheerful groom.

Beneath a spreading tree a man in white,
surrounded by his gathering of friends,
salutes the celebration of their love.
The merry feast grows more exuberant.
The shouts and songs ring through the winding streets
and echo in the distant fertile fields.

The day grows late, and still the feast persists,
the white-robed guest delighting in the bliss
of man and wife united under God.
A murmur like a breeze sweeps through the crowd.
His mother whispers, "Son, they have no wine."
He stands, his calloused hands take on their power.
His gesture indicates the rough stone urns,
commands that they be filled from Jordan's springs.
As water touches stone, it is transformed,
transmuted from a simple drink to wine,
the crimson burst of joy from Cana's grapes.

Communion

The water from the Jordan fills the Sea
and blesses Galilee's fertility .
Its wave had lapped the Baptist as he stood
and watched the dove descend upon the head
of he whose touch turns water into wine.

The grapes of Cana drink from Jordan's spring,
transform the vital waters to the juice
that flows forth to become the heady wine
that wedding guests now drink to toast the bride.
As wine and water mingle and transmute
in a communion, turning each to each,
so man and wife unite, body and soul,
in matrimony, sacramentalized
at Cana in the simple wedding feast.

Knowing Where Your Shoes Are

Your tennis shoes, tongues lolling,
sprawl on the floor.
Black patent pumps, heels primly together,
know their place in the closet:
beside dress boots, self-assured
in sophisticated ease.
Your slippers snuggle underneath the bed,
peeping from beneath the comforter.

Knowing where your shoes are:
knowing you in all your moves and moods,
all the ways you walk the erth
(striding, dancing, lingering):
knowing all the easy intimacies
that are the soul of love.

Swan Song

A sudden April rain—
we dash, drenched and laughing,
into a coffee shop.
Steaming cups of cappuccino
  make froth mustaches on our lips,
as we bet kisses on the race
    of raindrops
                coursing
        down
                    window glass.
We read each other poetry—
Dickinson and Frost—
and write haiku and limericks on notebook paper,
        which we shape into origami forms,
yours in pristine Swan Lake forms,
        mine bedraggled Pegasus.

The clouds chase toward the horizon
        as thunder tumbles off into the distance.
We emerge into the crystal air
and launch our verses
        among the rain-plucked petals
to float on the serendipitous stream
from the impromptu rain.
The folded figures pirouette
through pollen clouds
        (spent seed of languid flowers),
the gold dust double gilt
            by the Midas
of the returning sun.

Petals, pollen, and origami shapes

swirl toward the grinning maw
of the sewer grate
as folded wings and necks dip
           in watery defeat.
The hesitate, peering into the dark,
before the democratic flood
        sweeps all into its Stygian depths.
We shrug and smile at temporality,
        then stroll up the petal-littered sidewalk
beneath the dripping trees.

The Seasons of Love
(an epithalamion)

WINTER

The year dawns bleak, beneath the tarnished sun.
Gray, laden clouds disperse a sift of snow,
a sweep of desolate forgetfulness
that tucks the dormant seeds in drifting dreams.
The ice-bound branches chatter in the wind,
as silent sparrows shiver in the trees.
The starving fox pursues the rabbit's scent,
and life and warmth are distant memories.
So loneliness is winter in the heart.
The day dawns, dreary, desolate, and cold,
and strident banshee winds shriek out their loss.
The ice-edged teeth assail the forlorn soul
that shrouds itself in mute oblivion.

SPRING

The pirouetting Earth spins 'round the Sun;
Spring follows their celestial pas de deux.
The distant memory of life revives,
freed from the clutch of death's frigidity.
Beneath the thawing soil, insentient roots
recall the long-forgotten throb of life.
The tight-clenched knots of buds on barren trees
burst forth with life beneath the brooding Sun.
The harmonies of joyful robins' songs
call flowers forth from swelling fertile soil,
and ardent memories of vital heat
thaw winter's cold amnesia, flowing forth

in riotous profusion, perfumed sprays.
Thus love springs forth from numbing loneliness,
as passion's glow thaws winter in the soul.
Emotions long forgotten bloom within,
in fragrant harmonies of bridal song.

SUMMER

Spring's fragrant blossoms bud to summer fruits,
that ripen into nectarous luxury
beneath the sultry heat of solstice sun.
The air throbs with cicada's amorous buzz,
as breezes waft intoxicating scents,
and birds sing from the depth of verdant glades.
the summer afternoons drift like the clouds,
beneath the haze of summer's swelling heat.
Love's blossoms grow and ripen from the warmth
of passion's rising summer in the soul.
Love's warmth, like nectar, flows through trembling limbs;
each breath exhales the fertile, sweet perfume,
the honeyed, heady scent of love's delight.

AUTUMN

The sun's rays lengthen; supple, golden light
gilds apples, ripens fields of gleaming grain.
The vineyard grapes, replete with ruby wine,
drip, pendulous, from tendrils, intertwined.
The wheeling birds trill migratory songs;
their madrigals intone the turning year.
The harvest bounty fills the granaries,
the year fulfilled in autumn's gentle blush.

Thus, love fills and fulfills the waiting heart.
The fruits of passion ripen in the glow
of deeper love. Exuberant desires,
tempered to mellow fruitfulness, entwine,
abundant in the harvest of the heart.
Love's seasons sweep from winter's bitter freeze
to fertile lushness of the harvest swell.
a marriage is a harmony of hearts,
committed to the heat of brimming life
that winter's icy touch can never chill
through years and through the seasons of your love.

Beginning at Christmas

Beneath the erected tree—
blazing with the pagan promise
of eternal life, renewed
and evergreen—
we unwrap one another
like gifts.
To celebrate this Season of Love
and joy, we come
to one another with our offerings.
Lacking the Magi's exotic gifts—
gold, frankincense, and myrrh—
we offer up ourselves.
Mistletoe strains
to cover our passion with its power.
At the year's ending
and beginning, we meet
to celebrate our own ends
and beginnings.
Love, not recycled but renewed,
glows like kindled embers
on the blazing yule,
denying the deadly cold
of apathy and winter air.
To celebrate the birth
of gods and years,
we rise beneath the tree
to change with the year
and to renew
our belief in love.

Our Anniversary
(for Deloris)

The quiet joys of every day,
the warmth and love of every night,
are flowers in a bright bouquet
that fill us with delight.

The days and weeks turn into years,
the years of love we share:
a garden of joys and happiness,
of flowers sweet and rare.

As we walk on the garden paths
and share each fragrant bloom,
our love is like the sunlight
that keeps away the gloom.

Madame Butterfly II

Delicately clad in pastel hues,
Enchanting in her prima donna grace,
Like a flower freed, she wanders, if she choose,
On fairy-dusted wings of fragile lace.
Resting on a petal's pouting lip,
Iridescent in the golden summer light,
She tastes the nectar with a gentle sip.

Butterfly, your dance is a delight.
Radiant and free upon the breeze,
On wings of gossamer, as light as air,
Wafted by the wind, you dance with ease,
Not touched by any taint of mortal care.

Can any catch the rainbow's arching glow,
Or hold a shaft of sunlight in his hand?
Violet-winged, in royal robes you flow,
Ethereal as the breeze your wings have fanned,
Lifting your beauty up from far below.

Love among the Funnies

The waking sun slips through drawn blinds,
flows into the room,
oozes honey-butter yellow,
over carpet, comforter, and cushion.
Dust motes minuet on a golden shaft
that eludes the latticing slats
to spotlight the worn tray
laden with Sunday breakfast fare.

Two hefty ceramic mugs
(gold-glazed by the sun)
exhale their steaming sweetness
like a lover's open-mouthed kiss.
Delicate pastries, recumbent on a china plate,
nestle, front to back:
a sticky-sweet flow of marmalade
exudes from fragile folds.

The Sunday paper rests upon the bed,
its pristine pages sheathed
in polyethylene,
the sections all in order, neatly stacked.
The pages await familiar hands
that fumble between the sheets.
Sports page and fashion page
tumble to the floor and are strewn
in conjugal collusion.

A neglected gulp of coffee
chills in a cold stone mug.
A smear of marmalade congeals
and leaves a sugar-crusted stain

on the crumb-strewn porcelain plate.

The sunlight shifts across the floor,
retreats from comforter,
withdraws its warmth to window sill
and slides silently from the room.
The room cools in the changing light.
The bed is made, the dishes cleared,
the paper stacked.
The room, restored to order, waits
for other sunny Sundays,
another lingering dalliance
in honey-swirled moments
of love among the funnies.

Acknowledgements

I wish to thank the following people:

My family, friends, students, and colleagues who have encouraged me through the years; Mrs. Elsie Landess, my fifth and sixth grade teacher for whom I wrote my first poem; the Carrollton Creative Writers Club (and especially the Just Poetry group) for their help and encouragement; Diana Black for the cover design; Dr. Eleanor Wolfe Hoomes for her proofreading and her encouragement; Dr. Virginia Spencer Carr, my dissertation advisor, mentor and friend at Georgia State University; and my wife Deloris.

Made in the USA
Lexington, KY
26 September 2012